HiNDU FESTiVALS COOKBOOK

KERENA MARCHANT
WiTH PHOTOGRAPHY BY ZUL MUKHiDA

RAINTREE
STECK-VAUGHN
PUBLISHERS

A Harcourt Company

Austin   New York
www.steck-vaughn.com

Holiday Cookbooks
from Around the World

Christian Cookbook
Hindu Cookbook
Jewish Cookbook
Chinese Cookbook

Note: Nuts are contained in some of the recipes in this book
(see pages 18–19, 20, 24–25, 26–27, 28).
Nuts may provoke a dangerous allergic reaction in some people.

Published by Raintree Steck-Vaughn Publishers,
an imprint of Steck-Vaughn Company

Library of Congress Cataloging-in-Publication Data
Marchant, Kerena.
Hindu festivals cookbook / Kerena Marchant.
    p.   cm.–(Holiday cookbooks from around the world)
    Includes bibliographical references and index.
    ISBN 0-7398-3264-6
    1. Hindu cookbook–Juvenile literature.
    [1. Hindu cookbook.]
    I. Title.

Picture acknowledgments:

Art Directors and TRIP 6 (H. Rogers), 22, 23 (H. Rogers); Eye Ubiquitous 5 (David Cumming); Impact Photos 4 (Mohamed Ansar), 13 (Christopher Cormack), 14 (Mohamed Ansar), 21 (Mohamed Ansar), 29 (Christopher Cormack); Christine Osborne Pictures 15; Gettyone/Stone 7 (Paul Harris).

Printed in Italy. Bound in the United States.
1 2 3 4 5 6 7 8 9 0 05 04 03 02 01

Contents

HINDU FESTIVALS AND FOOD

The Hindu religion started in India. Hindus believe in one god, but worship that god in many different forms. The main forms are Vishnu, Shiva, the Goddess Shakti, Prince Rama, and Krishna. Because there are so many gods, there are many Hindu festivals during a year. They celebrate the birthdays or deeds of the gods.

Food plays a big part in Hindu worship. During festivals, the worshipers offer the gods' or goddesses' favorite foods to them and then share it among themselves. Most of the gods are believed to have a sweet tooth, so sweet foods and desserts often are a feature on the menu at festivals.

The gods are not fed at festivals alone. Before sitting down to a meal, Hindus offer some of the food they are about to eat to the gods. This food is called *prashad*. In the home, it is placed before the pictures or statues of the gods.

When Hindus visit a temple, they always bring *prashad* with them, especially at festival time.

Hindus are mostly vegetarian and do not eat meat. This is because Hindus believe in reincarnation: that when they die they are reborn as another human being or even an animal, bird, fish, or insect. To eat an animal or a bird might mean eating the soul of a human being about to be reborn.

The cow is regarded as a holy animal because the god Krishna loved cows. A Hindu will never kill a cow or wear leather that comes from a cow. Milk and dairy products are believed to have strong spiritual powers and are always offered to the gods at festivals.

Traditional Hindus will eat only food that has been cooked by them, their immediate family, or close friends. On a trip, they will eat only food that they have prepared. When Hindus emigrated from India, they continued to eat their traditional food. They did not eat the food of the countries where they went to live. That is why Hindu food remains the same all over the world.

Hindus eat meals with their right hands, instead of using cutlery. At this wedding feast in India, the food has been served on banana leaves.

SAFETY AND HYGIENE

When cutting with knives, frying, boiling, and using the oven, ALWAYS ask an adult to help you.

Food must always be kept clean. Food that gets dirty will not taste good—and can even make people sick.

Always wash your hands before you start cooking.

Do not wipe dirty hands on a towel. Wash your hands first.

If you need to taste something while cooking, use a clean fork or spoon.

Make sure work surfaces are clean and dry. This includes tables, countertops, and cutting boards.

HoLi

The Spring festival of Holi falls when there is a full moon in late February or early March, during the Hindu month of Phalguna. This joyous festival is celebrated throughout India, and everybody joins in.

The festival also celebrates the triumph of good over evil. People light huge bonfires to remember the time when the God Vishnu came down to earth as a man-lion. He saved his follower, Prahlad, from death in a bonfire and killed the evil tyrant who was tormenting him. In many villages, women carry their children around a bonfire asking Vishnu to protect them from evil in the months to come. Farmers may throw seeds on the bonfire and ask god to bless the crops that will be planted soon.

Holi is not a time to wear your best clothes. Everybody celebrates by throwing powdered dye and colored water at each other. This sticks to clothes and hair. It takes a great many baths and shampoos to get rid of it. Clothes are best thrown away after Holi! Paint is thrown as a symbol of the time that the god Krishna playfully threw paint over the milkmaids and they threw paint over Krishna and his friends.

In India, it is hard to avoid the dye-throwing in the street during Holi.

Revelers with colored dye and water visit many houses. One way to avoid opening the door to a faceful of paint is to have plenty of snacks and hot drinks ready to feed the hungry revelers. The following pages show you how to make the kinds of foods that are often eaten in India during the Holi celebrations.

Making treats for Holi in Jaipur, India. The most popular cooking method in India is frying in a deep pan called a *karhai*. The word "curry" comes from *karhai*.

Samosas

Preparation time: 1 hour

Cooking time: 20 to 30 minutes

Oven temperature: 375°F

Makes: 20 samosas

Ingredients

1/2 lb potatoes

1 oz carrots (about 1/2 a carrot)

2 tbsp ghee, clarified butter, or vegetable oil

2 pinches ground turmeric

1/2 tsp chili powder (optional)

1 tsp salt

2 tsp garam masala (spice)

3/4 cup frozen peas, thawed

20 sheets of filo (phyllo) pastry, cut into rectangles about 12 inches x 6 inches

Small bowl of oil for brushing filo pastry

Equipment

Saucepan

Chef's knife

Cutting board

Mixing bowl

Pastry brush

Cookie sheet

Samosas are triangle-shaped packets of food. Hindus fill them with vegetables; other people may use meat as well. They are a popular snack in many parts of the world and can be eaten hot or cold. Usually they are deep-fried, but this recipe cooks them in an oven, which is much safer.

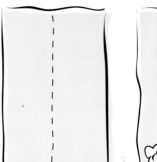
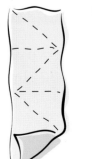

1 Peel the potatoes and carrots. Ask an adult to boil them for 5 minutes, so that they are partly cooked. Drain and let them cool down. Cut them into small pieces.

2 Put the vegetables into a bowl. Add the ghee, butter, or oil, turmeric, chili powder (if using), salt, garam masala, and peas. Stir well to mix.

3 Take a sheet of filo pastry, and brush half of the strip with oil. Fold it in half lengthwise, and brush one corner with the oil.

4 Put 2 teaspoons of the vegetable mixture on the oiled end of the pastry, and fold the pastry over diagonally, to make a triangle.

5 Fold the triangle over and over until all the pastry is used up. (See diagram, left.)

6 Place the samosas on an oiled cookie sheet, and brush the tops with plenty of oil. Ask an adult to bake them for 20 to 30 minutes in the oven.

9

Onion Bhajis

Preparation time: 10 minutes

Cooking time: 20 minutes

Makes: 4 large bhajis

Ingredients

3 large onions

7 tbsp vegetable oil

1 tsp mustard seeds

1/2 tsp ground turmeric

1/3 cup chickpea (garbanzo) or cornmeal flour

1/2 tsp salt

1/2 tsp chili powder (optional)

Equipment

Chef's knife

Wooden spoon

Frying pan

Spatula

These fried onion cakes (bhajis, pronounced "bah-jees") are eaten as a snack. People take them to eat on journeys or prepare them for unexpected guests. A plentiful supply of bhajis is a must at Holi. Normally, bhajis are deep-fried, but these are shallow-fried for safety reasons.

1 Ask an adult to help you slice the onions.

2 Fry the mustard seeds and turmeric in 4 tablespoons of the oil until the seeds begin to pop.

3 Turn down the heat. Add the sliced onions, and fry gently for another 10 minutes, until the onions are soft.

4 Add 1 tablespoon of the chickpea flour or cornmeal and stir. Do this again until all the flour has been used up.

5 Add the salt and chili powder, (or some pepper if you don't use the chili powder).

6 Take the mixture off the stove to cool down. When it is cool, divide it into 4 pieces, and mold each piece into a ball. Flatten the balls.

7 Ask an adult to heat the remaining oil and fry the bhajis, until they are brown all over. Use a spatula to make sure they don't fall apart.

Garam Doodh

Cooking time: 10 minutes

Makes: 2 mugs

Ingredients

2 1/2 cups milk

2 tbsp honey

Pinch of grated nutmeg

Equipment

Saucepan

Spoon

This hot milk drink warms revelers on a cold Holi night. Festivals, such as Holi, that celebrate stories about Krishna, always involve food and drinks made from dairy products. Milk, butter, and yogurt were Krishna's favorite food and drink.

1 Put the milk in the pan, and ask an adult to bring it to a boil.

2 Let the milk simmer for 5 minutes, without boiling over.

3 Take the milk off the heat, and stir in the honey and nutmeg.

4 Pour carefully into mugs, and serve.

OTHeR HOLi CeLeBRaTiONS

The spirit of Holi celebrations takes over India, with many people joining in. Outside India this does not happen. In other countries, the Hindu communities do not have widespread Holi revels, since not everybody is Hindu, and most people would not welcome having paint thrown at them in the street!

The best Holi celebrations in the Western world are at ISKCON (Krishna Consciousness) centers. The statues of Krishna in the temple are dressed in festival clothes. Before the festival begins, members of the community spend hours in the kitchen preparing Krishna's favorite foods, which they offer to the statues in the temple and to people coming to join in the festivities. There is worship in the temple, and revelers throw paint outside. In the evening there are plays about Krishna, his life among the milkmaids and cowherds, and the times he saved the world from evil.

During Holi celebrations in England, people cook coconuts in the traditional bonfire.

13

Divali

Divali means "row of lights," and Divali is the Hindu festival of light. It falls in the Hindu month of Kartika, which can occur either in October or November, depending on the cycle of the moon. Divali is celebrated all over India, and by Hindus in many other countries. Different stories and gods are remembered in different areas.

At Divali, Hindus draw colorful *rangoli* patterns using dyed rice flour.

A Hindu pastry store sells hundreds of boxes of candy each day before Divali.

Some people celebrate the time when Prince Rama was crowned king of Ayodhya after killing the evil tyrant Ravana. When Rama returned to his kingdom, the roads were dark and people lit lamps at all the houses to guide him on his way.

Most people associate Divali with the Goddess of Fortune, Lakshmi. Everyone wants Lakshmi to visit his or her home at Divali to bring good fortune for the year to come. No effort is spared to entice her into the house. Houses are spring cleaned from top to bottom. Clay lanterns called *diwas* are lit at every door and window. Houses, stores, and temples are strung with colored lights.

Food plays an important part in the Divali festivities and sweet foods are prepared to exchange as gifts. Snacks are made to feed visitors calling with Divali cards and gifts. It is a time when families get together to feast and attend grand firework displays. These family feasts go on long into the night after the fireworks have finished.

Mattar Paneer

Preparation time: 10 minutes

Cooking time: 30 minutes

Serves: 6 to 8

Ingredients

10 oz paneer or mozzarella

6 tbsp vegetable oil

2 onions

1 cup water

1/2 tsp salt

1 lb frozen peas, thawed

1 tsp sugar

2 tsp ground turmeric

1/2 tsp chili powder

2 tsp dried ginger

1 tbsp fresh chopped coriander (or parsley)

Equipment

Frying pan

Wooden spoon

Chef's knife

Cutting board

Paper towel

Measuring cup

No festival vegetarian meal is complete without this dish of spiced vegetables and Indian cheese. Some people make a fresh batch of paneer every day to use in dishes such as this one, and in desserts. Paneer can be bought in Indian shops and some supermarkets. If you can't find it, you can use Italian mozzarella.

1 Cut the paneer into small cubes. Ask an adult to fry it in the oil until brown. Stir the cheese pieces so they get brown all over and don't stick to the pan.

2 When the cheese is brown, take it out of the frying pan. Put it on a piece of paper towel to drain. Leave the rest of the oil in the pan.

3 Chop the onions fine. Ask an adult to put them in the pan and fry for 3 to 4 minutes, stirring all the time.

4 Add the water and salt and bring the mixture to a boil.

5 Add the peas and sugar and cover. Turn the heat down to a simmer. Cook the mixture for 10 minutes.

6 Add the paneer, turmeric, chili, and ginger and simmer for another 10 minutes, uncovered.

7 Put the mattar paneer in a serving dish and sprinkle the coriander over the top.

Pulao Rice with Peas and Nuts

Preparation time: 10 minutes

Cooking time: 30 minutes

Serves: 6 to 8

Ingredients

$2/3$ cup basmati rice

4 tbsp ghee, clarified butter, or oil

1 tsp cumin seeds

1 medium onion, sliced

4 cloves

1 tsp ground cinnamon

1 tsp garam masala

$1/2$ tsp salt

half of a 10-oz package frozen peas

$1/4$ cup cashew nuts

$1/4$ cup raisins

1 cup water

Equipment

Large bowl

Strainer

Large saucepan with a heavy bottom

Wooden spoon

Festive meals usually include pulao rice. The word "pulao" (pronounced "poolow") describes the method of cooking rice with vegetables and spices. The best rice to use for this dish is basmati rice. It stays light and fluffy, provided it is washed before cooking to get rid of extra starch that would make it sticky. Pulao rice goes well with the Mattar Paneer.

1 Put the rice in a bowl and carefully rinse in water. The water will get cloudy. Change the water a few times. When the water is clear, leave the rice to drain in a strainer.

2 Ask an adult to heat the ghee, butter, or oil in the saucepan with the cumin seeds.

3 After 3 minutes add the onion, cloves, and cinnamon. Fry gently until the onion is brown.

4 Add the rice and cook for 2 minutes to get rid of the remaining water in the rice.

5 Stir in the garam masala, salt, peas, nuts, and raisins.

6 Pour in the water and bring to a boil. Turn down to a simmer, stir, and cover the saucepan. Cook for 15 minutes. Take the pan off the heat and leave for 5 minutes, covered, before serving. This makes the rice nice and fluffy.

Coconut Barfi

Barfi (pronounced "barfee") is a popular Indian treat, which is always made for festivals. It's usually made by boiling sugar and milk together. This recipe is much easier to make, and is just as good.

Preparation time: 20 minutes

Makes: 20 pieces

Ingredients

¹/₃ cup honey

8 tbsp peanut butter

10 to 12 dates, chopped fine

A 1-quart envelope (3.2 oz) non-fat dry milk

1¹/₃ cup shredded coconut

5 tps rose water, (optional)

Equipment

Large mixing bowl

Small mixing bowl

Waxed paper

Chef's knife

Cookie tin

1 Mix the honey, peanut butter, dates, and powdered milk in a bowl using your hands. Make the sticky mixture into a non-sticky dough by kneading it. (Or ask an adult to mix the ingredients in a food processor.)

2 Roll the dough into a log about 20 inches long. Now wash your sticky hands and dry them well.

3 In the small mixing bowl, mix the coconut and the rose water, or plain water.

4 Spread out the coconut and rose-water mixture on the waxed paper.

5 Cut the log in half, and roll each half in the coconut so that it covers the log.

6 Cut each log into 10 pieces and store in the cookie tin. It will keep for about a week in the refrigerator. It tastes best if you take it out of the refrigerator about an hour before eating it.

OTHER DIVALI CELEBRATIONS

Hindus living outside India celebrate Divali with a flourish as it brings people together. The houses, stores, and temples in Hindu areas are lit using clay lamps and colored lights. Hindu temples become the focus for the celebrations. People travel great distances to celebrate Divali at the temple, and to meet family and friends who live a long way away.

Huge meals are prepared at Hindu temples for the large number of worshipers at Divali.

One of the best Divali celebrations is on the Caribbean island of Trinidad. Everybody on the island, even people who are not Hindu, such as Muslims and Christians, join in the celebrations. Divali becomes a carnival. The streets and buildings are lit, there are carnival processions, and steel bands play on into the night. Stands along the carnival route sell Caribbean food—curried goat and jerk chicken—as well as traditional Hindu snacks and curries.

Ganesh Chaturthi

This festival celebrates the birth of the elephant-headed god, Ganesh. It is said that Ganesh can remove any obstacles one might face. The festival is celebrated in late August or early September, which is during the Hindu month of Bhadra. Ganesh is a popular god, and this festival is celebrated throughout India. It can last as long as seven to ten days.

A Ganesh festival procession in Hyderabad, India

This painting of Ganesh shows him holding a bowl of his favorite treat, ladoos.

During the festival, worshipers make a giant statue of Ganesh. The statue is paraded around a town and taken to a place where everyone can see it. Worshipers bring offerings of Ganesh's favorite foods. At the end of the festival, the statue is sunk in the sea, a lake, or a river.

Everybody knows the story of Ganesh's favorite foods. Ganesh always travels in a chariot driven by a mouse. One night, Ganesh's mouse was frightened by a snake, and the god fell out of his chariot. When he fell, his stomach burst open and the last food he had eaten—sweet rice pudding and ladoos (round sweet balls)—fell out. The moon laughed at Ganesh. This made the god angry. He tied up the hole in his stomach with the snake and cursed the moon. This story explains why the moon does not stay full all the time, but waxes and wanes.

During the festival, worshipers avoid looking at the moon for fear of offending Ganesh.

Kheer

Cooking time: 20 minutes

Oven temperature: 275°F

Serves: 6

Ingredients

1 lb ready-made rice pudding, OR, to make your own, use:

   1/3 cup short grain rice

   5 cups milk

   2 tbsp brown sugar

To continue:

1 cup milk

1/4 cup golden raisins

1 tbsp chopped almonds

1 tbsp ground or crushed pistachios

1/2 tsp ground cardamom

1 tbsp sugar

1 tsp rose water (optional)

Extra pistachios for decoration

Equipment

Oven casserole

Saucepan

Spoon

Serving dish

Try this sweet rice pudding, even if you don't like puddings. The spices make it taste wonderful! No wonder Ganesh, who had a sweet tooth, found it irresistible.

1 If you want to make the rice pudding from scratch, make it in the oven: put the rice, 2½ cups milk, and 2 tbsp brown sugar into a heatproof casserole. Put it in the oven for 3 hours. After 1 hour, ask an adult to stir the pudding and add 1¼ cups more milk. After 2 hours, add another 1¼ cups milk.

2 Put a cup of milk into a saucepan. Carefully add the rice pudding (homemade or from the store). Ask an adult to bring it to a boil.

3 Add the raisins, almonds, pistachios, cardamom, and sugar. Bring back to a boil.

Note: If you can't buy pistachios already ground, wrap a tablespoon of the nuts in waxed paper and crush them using a rolling pin. They don't have to be fine-ground.

4 Reduce the heat and simmer the mixture for about 6 minutes, stirring so it does not stick.

5 Remove from the heat and stir in the rose water (optional).

6 Put the mixture into a serving dish. Decorate the rice pudding by putting ground or chopped pistachio nuts on top. Eat it hot or cold.

Ladoos

Cooking time: 1 hour

Makes: 12 to 15 balls

Ingredients

$\frac{1}{2}$ lb butter (2 sticks)

2 cups chickpea flour (also called garbanzo flour)

$1\frac{1}{2}$ tbsp grated/dried coconut

$1\frac{1}{2}$ tbsp chopped walnuts or hazelnuts

$\frac{1}{2}$ tsp ground cardamom or cinnamon

1 cup confectioners' sugar

Equipment

Frying pan

Wooden spoon

Fork

Ladoos are sweet balls made of sugar, butter, and flour. They are a popular treat, and a batch of these does not last long. Ganesh had eaten quite a number of ladoos when he fell out of his chariot.

1 Put the butter into the frying pan and ask an adult to melt it over low heat.

2 Add the chickpea flour and stir with a wooden spoon over gentle heat for 15 minutes to toast the flour. It is toasted when it has a nutty smell.

3 Stir in the coconut, the nuts, and the cardamom or cinnamon. Fry for another 2 minutes and stir to mix in all the ingredients.

4 Take the pan off the heat. Add the sugar and mix well with a fork so there are no lumps. Leave to cool.

5 When the mixture is cool, moisten your hands and roll the mixture into 12 or 15 balls about 1½ inches in diameter.

Scented Almond Drink

Ganesh Chaturthi occurs during the hot Indian summer and cool drinks are welcome both as offerings for Ganesh and for worshipers. Milk, or milk-like drinks, are thought to have spiritual qualities. This is why they are popular at festivals.

Preparation time: 1 hour

Cooking time: 20 minutes

Makes: 6 drinks

Ingredients

2/3 cup blanched almonds

1/2 tsp cardamom seeds

4 whole peppercorns

2 cups boiling water

4 tbsp honey

2 cups white grape juice

1/2 tbsp rose water (optional)

2 cups still or sparkling mineral water

Equipment

Mixing bowl

Measuring cup

Electric blender

Strainer

Cheesecloth

Pitcher

1 Put the almonds, cardamom seeds, and peppercorns into a bowl. Add 1 1/4 cups of boiling water and leave to soak for an hour.

2 After an hour put the mixture into a blender and, with an adult's help blend it into a fine paste.

3 Add the honey and another 3/4 cup of boiling water and blend again.

4 Put the strainer over a pitcher or bowl. Line the strainer with cheesecloth, and pour the mixture through the cheesecloth. The nut mixture will remain in the cheesecloth: you don't need this anymore.

5 Pour the "nut milk" into a pitcher. Add the grape juice, mineral water, and rose water, and stir.

6 Put the pitcher into the refrigerator to chill before serving.

OTHER GANESH CHATURTHI CELEBRATIONS

Like so many Indian festivals outside India, Ganesh Chaturthi is a simple affair. Hindus visit their nearest temple to pay their respects to the statue of Ganesh. Hindu temples can be quite modest in countries other than India. Many are ordinary houses where one room is made into a temple. In areas where there is a large Hindu population, there might be a larger temple.

In India, temples are usually dedicated to one of the gods. In other countries, the different gods may share a temple. For some Hindus who live a long way from their nearest temple, the festival will be celebrated in the home. Most Hindu homes have a statue or picture of Ganesh as well as of other gods.

Making elephant masks for festival celebrations

The gods are part of the family. They will be offered food before the family eats, and prayers will be said. Before making a journey, family members will always ask Ganesh's blessing. During the festival, family members will offer the statue or picture of Ganesh the ladoos, rice pudding, coconut, and a drink as well as gifts of flowers.

FURTHER INFORMATION

The three festivals covered in this book are just a few of the many Hindu festivals celebrated in India, often at different times of the year. Other festivals include Maha Shiva Ratri (in honor of Shiva), Sarasvati Puja (first day of Spring), Rama Naumi (Rama's birthday), Ratha Yatra (in honor of Vishnu), Janmashtami (the birth of Krishna), and Navaratri (celebrating Durga). There are also many local festivals that are specific to a particular area.

When using the recipes contained in this book, children should be supervised by one or more adults at all times. This especially applies when cutting with knives, cooking on the stovetop, and using the oven.

EQUIPMENT
The recipes are written on the understanding that adults have access to weighing and measuring equipment such as scales and measuring cups. For clarity, these have not been shown in photos.

The traditional pan for frying Indian food is a *karhai,* which looks like a Chinese wok with a thick bottom. Using a wok or a *karhai* with children is not always a good idea as they are easy to tip over during cooking. A thick-bottomed frying pan will be safer and easier to use.

Indian food is served on *thali* dishes. These are small bowls on a large tray. If you cannot find these, it is easy to improvise, using dessert bowls on a large tray.

Hindus eat meals with the right hand instead of using cutlery. The left hand is used for personal hygiene, including going to the toilet. It's important to wash before eating.

COOKING METHODS
The traditional Hindu method of cooking snacks such as samosas and onion bhajis is to deep-fry them in the *karhai.* For safety reasons, in this book they have been shallow-fried or cooked in the oven. Sweet snacks such as barfi are normally boiled using a mixture of hot sugar, water, and powdered milk.

Samosas: initially, the way of wrapping the triangles may seem rather complicated, but it is easily mastered, with practice. See the diagram on page 8.

Chili powder is optional in recipe, since some children don't like hot food. If you do use chili, stress the safety aspect of working with it. Children must not touch the chili and then put their hands to their eyes. If this happens, rinse out the eye liberally with water.

INGREDIENTS
Note: Nuts, contained in some recipes in this book, may provoke a severe allergic reaction in some people.

Rice: Always try to use basmati rice in Hindu cooking. It stays separated after cooking and does not become heavy or gluey like other kinds of rice.

Ghee: Use this for cooking if you can. Ghee is clarified butter. You can make your own clarified butter by melting butter, skimming any foam, and pouring off the clear butter, discarding the milk solids. Clarified butter and ghee can be heated to a high temperature without risk of burning. However, if you prefer, use vegetable oil instead.

Paneer: (can also be spelled panier) This is Indian curd cheese. It is made by curdling milk, separating the white curds, and pressing them into a cheese. It is sometimes sold already cut into pieces, and sometimes as a whole piece. If you can't find this, use mozzarella. If you use paneer be careful since it spoils very quickly. It also sticks very easily to the skillet: be sure to stir it constantly while frying.

Chickpea (garbanzo) flour: This is made from ground chickpeas and can be bought in Indian stores. It is pale yellow and has a sweet, nutty flavor. It is best to use this for ladoos if at all possible, but if you cannot buy it, an alternative may be cornmeal.

Garam masala: A ready-made mixture of spices (cardamon, cinnamon, cloves, cumin, coriander, and black peppercorns).

GLOSSARY

Cowherds People who look after a small number of cows.

Dairy Describes foods made from animals' milk, such as cheese, yogurt, and butter.

Emigrate To leave one's own country and go to live in another country.

Ganesh The elephant-headed god who removes obstacles from the path of religious life.

Karhai A Hindu frying pan. It looks like a Chinese wok.

Krishna An incarnation of the God Vishnu. Krishna was brought up in a village with cowherds and milkmaids. He loves cows and food made from dairy products such as milk, butter, and yogurt.

Paneer Indian curd cheese.

Prashad Sacred food that is offered to the gods.

Rama One of the incarnations of Vishnu, who appeared as an Indian prince.

Rangoli **patterns** Brightly colored patterns made with rice flour that are used to decorate pathways at Divali. The patterns are usually of sacred Hindu symbols and flowers.

Reincarnation Being reborn after death as another human, animal, bird, fish, or insect.

Spices Vegetable extracts used to flavor food, such as chili, turmeric, and ginger.

Statue A figure of a god, person, or animal. Statues can be made out of materials such as stone, metal, wood, or clay and painted with colors.

Temple A building where a god or gods are worshiped.

Thali A selection of small bowls placed on a large tray.

Hindus often eat their food from a *thali*.

Tyrant A cruel ruler.

Vegetarian Somebody who does not eat meat or fish.

Vishnu One of the three most important Hindu gods. He is the protector of the world and is often considered God himself.

INDEX

Page numbers in **bold** refer to photographs

RESOURCES

Deshpande, Chris. *Diwali.* A & C Black, 1998.

Godden, Rumer. *Premlata and the Festival of Lights.* HarperCollins Juvenile, 1999.

Kadodwala, Dilip. *Divali.* Raintree Steck-Vaughn, 1998.

Kadodwala, Dilip. *Holi.* Raintree Steck-Vaughn, 1998.

MacMillan, Dianne M. *Diwali: Hindu Festival of Lights.* Enslow, 1997.